Longman English Guides

ABC of Common Errors

S H Burton

Longman

Titles in the series

ABC of Common Errors *S H Burton*

Writing Letters *S H Burton*

Punctuation *Ian Gordon*

Spelling *S H Burton*

Help Yourself to Study *Lesley Millard Ralph Tabberer*

LONGMAN GROUP UK LIMITED
Longman House
Burnt Mill, Harlow, Essex CM20 2JE, England
and Associated Companies throughout the World.

© Longman Group Limited 1983

First published 1983
Fourth impression 1986

ISBN 0-582-25053-6

Set in 10/11pt Linotron Rockwell Light and Medium

Produced by Longman Group (FE) Ltd
Printed in Hong Kong

CONTENTS

Introduction

Mistakes that people often make are dealt with in this little book. It is a quick guide, arranged alphabetically so that you can easily look up any point on which you need help. The explanations are all given in commonsense and everyday language so it is a book you can use on your own. I hope you will find it a useful – and cheerful – companion when you are writing.

S H Burton

A

A

1 a *or* an?

Whether *a* is right or *an* is right depends upon the sound of the first letter of the next word.

wrong

1 Even in *a airy* room, non-smokers find tobacco smoke unpleasant.
2 The train arrived nearly *a hour* late.
3 The complicated rules got us into *an horrible* tangle.
4 The mayor described the team's success as *an unique* achievement.
5 She inherited those books from *a uncle*, her mother's brother.

right

1 an airy room
2 an hour
3 a horrible tangle
4 a unique achievement
5 an uncle

REMEMBER the rules for using *a* or *an*:

- Use *an* before a word beginning with a vowel — an airy room — an exciting day — an interesting story — an octopus — an unidentified flying object.
- Use *an* before a word beginning with a silent *h* —an hour — an honourable defeat — an honest statement.
- Use *a* before a word beginning with a consonant — a horrible tangle — a hard task — a bad choice — a rotten apple.

7

- Use *a* before a word beginning with *u* when the *u* is pronounced *yu* — a unique achievement — a united front — a union of peace-loving powers.

NOTE The vowels are: a e i o u. All the other letters in the alphabet are consonants except y: either a vowel (carrying) or a consonant (yellow).

2 actual/actually — and two other overworked words

Do not use *actual/actually*, *definite/definitely*, *real/really* unless you are sure that the word is needed to make your meaning clear.

wrong

1 The local paper reported that the race began at 2 o'clock, but in *actual* fact it began at 2.15.
2 We usually go away in August, but we are *definitely* going in July this year.
3 I was not *actually* aware that my colleagues knew it was my birthday, so it was a *real* surprise to find a card on my desk.
4 "Would you *really* recognise that man if you saw him again?"
"*Definitely*, yes."
5 The hours he is spending in the gym *definitely* prove that he is *really* determined to be fit when the championship matches *actually* begin.

right

1 Omit *actual*
2 Omit *definitely*
3 Omit *actually* and *real*

4 Omit *really* and *definitely*
5 Omit *definitely*, *really* and *actually*

A total of 9 wasted words in 5 sentences!

3 affect or effect?

These two words are often confused. Remember this sentence. It shows the *correct* use.

The cold summer badly *affected* the sales of soft drinks and so *effected* the collapse of the Mountain Mineral Water Company.

Explanation

When you *effect* something, you bring it about or accomplish it.

The prisoners effected their escape through the tunnel.

When an *effect* is produced on a person or thing, that person or thing is *affected* by it,

The effects of age affect us all in time.

4 all ready or already?

Use *all ready* when it refers to people or things.

Use *already* when it refers to actions.

wrong
1 The children were so eager to go to the circus that they were *already* before lunch.
2 Bill's father asked him to feed the cat, but Bill told him that he had *all ready* done so.

right
1 The children were so eager to go to the circus that they were all ready before lunch.
2 Bill's father asked him to feed the cat, but Bill told him that he had already done so.

Practice

Fill the gap in each of the following with either *all ready* or *already*.

1 I was going to tell my grandparents about my new job, but they — knew about it from my mother.
2 Some of the painting will have been done, but the decorators cannot promise to have the room — by Easter.

5 all right

REMEMBER There's no such word as *alright*. Always write *all right*!

6 all together or altogether?

They are used differently.

Use *all together* to describe people or things in a group or collection.

Use *altogether* when you mean "entirely" or "on the whole".

wrong

1 Jill is a tidy worker and keeps her woodcraft things *altogether*.
2 He didn't seem *all together* pleased when he heard the news.

right

1 Jill is a tidy worker and keeps her woodcraft things all together.
2 He didn't seem altogether pleased when he heard the news.

Practice

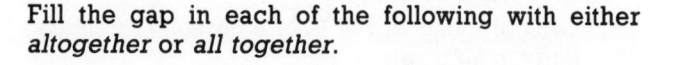

Fill the gap in each of the following with either *altogether* or *all together*.

1 The two families shared a holiday chalet last year, but it was not an — successful experiment.
2 It's not so bad when they leave the pub at intervals, but when they leave — they make a lot of noise.

7 amount *or* number?

Do not use *amount* when you mean *number*.

Amount applies to mass or bulk *not* to *numbers*.

wrong

1 How did Noah get such a large *amount* of animals into the Ark?
2 A considerable *amount* of students entered the exam last year.

right

1 How did Noah get such a large number of animals into the Ark?
2 A considerable number of students entered the exam last year.

A sentence to remember:

That greedy brat has eaten an enormous number of sweets, including a large amount of toffee.

11

8 anybody, anyone, nobody, no one, somebody, someone

Each of these words is *one* person (singular).
Body is singular.
One is singular.
So, commonsense tells us that *anybody, anyone, nobody, no one, somebody, someone* must each be singular.

wrong

1 Anybody *are* entitled to borrow extra books for the Christmas holidays if *they* fill in the special form.
2 Somebody stole a spare key, but we shall discover *their* identity because *they* left *their* fingerprints on the safe door.
3 Anyone who *enter* these competitions for the first time *stand* as good a chance of winning as those who have been competing for years.

right

1 Anybody is entitled to borrow extra books for the Christmas holidays if he fills in the special form.
2 Somebody stole a spare key, but we shall discover his identity because he left his fingerprints on the safe door.
3 Anyone who enters these competitions for the first time stands as good a chance of winning as those who have been competing for years.

Practice

Choose the correct word from inside the brackets to fill each gap in these sentences.

1 Somebody rushed up to the barrier, showed — (their/his) ticket, and dashed on to the platform to catch — (his/their) train.

2 Anybody is welcome to join who — (do/does) — (his/their) best to make — (themselves/himself) useful in running this club.
3 No one — (are/is) to blame — (themselves/himself) for this accident, for which nobody — (is/are) in any way personally responsible.

9 angry at/angry with

You are angry *at* things and events.

You are angry *with* people and animals.

A sentence to remember:

John's father was angry at the mess in the kitchen, but he was even angrier with his son for making it.

B

10 bulk (of) wrongly used for most (of) or majority (of)

Do not write *bulk (of)* when you are referring to *numbers (of)*.

wrong
1 When we elected the club secretary, the *bulk* of the votes went to Mary.
2 The *bulk* of the students in this age group are learning a foreign language.

right
1 — the majority of the votes —
2 Most of the students —

right
When the lorry driver braked sharply, the bulk of the load shifted forwards and crushed the cab.

11 but or and?

We often make two separate statements in one sentence.

Sometimes the sense of the sentence depends on using *but* between the two statements. For example:

She worked hard for the exam, but she failed.

Statement 1: She worked hard for the exam
          but ("turning point" between the two statements)

Statement 2: she failed.

Sometimes the sense of the sentence depends on using *and* between the two statements. For example:

She worked hard for the exam and she passed.

Statement 1: She worked hard for the exam
　　　　　　and ("link" between the two state-
　　　　　　ments)
Statement 2: she passed.

REMEMBER The sense of a sentence breaks down when a "turning point" (*but*) is confused with a "link" (*and*).

wrong
1　I admit this car is ten years old *and* it has been serviced regularly.
2　The jockey rode the race of his life *and* his horse was outclassed.
3　We dropped a second anchor *and* the boat still drifted.

right
　　Use *but* instead of *and* in each sentence.

wrong
1　It rained all night, *but* by morning our sleeping bags were soaked.
2　The subscription was doubled last year, *but* we lost several members who thought the new rate was too high.
3　The engineers have made a breakthrough, *but* they are near to success.

right
　　Use *and* instead of *but* in each sentence.

E

12 each

Each is singular. So, too, is *every*.
See **anybody**, **anyone**, etc. and follow the same rules.

wrong

1 Each pupil in these forms *are* taking *their* parents a mid-term report.
2 Every part-time female worker will get *their* bonus at Christmas.

right

1 Each pupil in these forms is taking his or her parents a mid-term report.
2 Every part-time female worker will get her bonus at Christmas.

13 each other/one another

Each other refers to two people or things.

One another refers to three or more people or things.

wrong

1 They are twins, but they are not at all like *one another*.
2 The spectators were shouting at the referee and arguing with *each other*.

right

    1 They are twins, but they are not at all like each other.

    2 The spectators were shouting at the referee and arguing with one another.

14 either

Use *either* to refer to one of *two* people or things.

When more than two people or things are involved, use *any* or *any one*.

wrong

    1 There were three trophies in the show case and the winners were allowed to choose *either*.

    2 Did you notice anything strange about the appearance of *either* of those four women in that room?

right

    1 There were three trophies in the show case and the winners were allowed to choose any one.

    2 Did you notice anything strange about the appearance of any of those four women in that room?

Neither, like *either*, refers to one of *two* people or things. When more than two are involved, use *none* or *not one*.

15 either — or/neither — nor/both — and

Each word of these "paired" words must be placed in its proper position in the sentence. If the two words are not "in balance" the sentence does not make sense.

wrong

1 The doctor *either* advised me to eat less *or* to take more exercise.
2 We discovered that, on Sundays, there *neither* was a train *nor* a convenient bus for the journey.
3 Candidates must *both* answer the first question in Section A *and* the first question in Section B.

right

1 The doctor advised me either to eat less or to take more exercise.
2 We discovered that, on Sundays, there was *neither* a train *nor* a convenient bus for the journey.
3 Candidates must answer both the first question in Section A and the first question in Section B.

Explanation

When you use these paired words, *either — or*, *neither — nor*, *both — and*, you set up a "two-track" sentence. Like this:

We were not certain either of the date or of the time of his arrival.

Here are the two "tracks":

We were not certain (either) of the date / (or) of the time \ of his arrival.

When the two parts of *either — or* are correctly placed, as in that example, the sentence "train" can run safely along either "track":

We were not certain (either) of the date of his arrival.
We were not certain (or) of the time of his arrival.

But, when *either — or*, *neither — nor*, *both — and* are in the wrong places, the sentence "train" is "derailed". Like this:

wrong

We were not either certain of the date or of the time of his arrival.

(either) certain of the date

We were not of his arrival.

(or) of the time

The "train" of that sentence cannot run safely along the bottom "track". When it tries to, there's a "crash": "We were not (or) of the time of his arrival."

Each "track" must be capable of carrying the sentence "train" safely to the end of its journey.

Practice

If you think that these sentences are wrong, put them right. Use the "two track" test if you are in doubt.

1 Nobody can both reasonably expect to spend all he earns and to increase his savings.
2 The intruders left empty-handed, for they either failed to find the safe or they were unable to open it.

16 every/everybody/everyone

These words refer to *one* person or thing (singular). See *anybody, anyone* for the rules.

right

1 Every girl in the race deserves credit for her effort.
2 Everybody on board is reminded that he or she must report for boat drill at 10 a.m.
3 A certificate will be awarded to everyone who completes the Course.

F

17 farther (farthest)/further (furthest)

To show distance use either *farther* or *further*.

To show an additional number or quantity use only *further*.

wrong
1 Wine with the meal involved her in *farther* expense.
2 The programme concluded with a *farther* warning of the dangers of re-heated food.

right
1 Wine with the meal involved her in further expense.
2 The programme concluded with a further warning of the dangers of re-heated food.
3 That was the furthest (or farthest) point reached by the expedition.
4 The scientist had pushed her experiments further (or farther) than was safe.

18 few or less?

See *less or few?*

19 (to be) finished/(to have) finished

They have different meanings. Don't confuse them.

Two sentences to remember:

"I am finished," gasped the exhausted runner, as he fell in the last lap.

"I have finished," gasped the exhausted runner, as he crossed the line.

F

wrong
1 *Are* you finished with those spanners?
2 You can have them back, now. *I'm* finished with them.

right
1 Have you finished with those spanners?
2 You can have them back, now. I've finished with them.

20 former

Former should be used only to refer to one of *two* persons or things.
See also *latter*.

wrong
1 Smith, Brown and Jones discussed the news at the *former's* house.
2 Offered a ticket for the theatre, a seat at Wimbledon, or a day at the races, Jill chose the *former*.

right
1 Smith, Brown and Jones discussed the news at Smith's house.
2 Offered a ticket for the theatre, a seat at Wimbledon, or a day at the races, Jill chose the first.

G

21 get/got/have got, etc.

Don't overwork these useful "getting" words. They can be used to express several different meanings, for example: achieving something, acquiring something, arriving somewhere, possessing something, being made to do something. They are often the shortest and most vigorous way of expressing those meanings. There *are* other words, however, and when you overdo the "getting" words, your writing is monotonous.

Practice

Without changing the sense of this passage, think of other words for some of the "getting" words. You need not remove all the "getting" words. Leave those that you think are the best for the writer's purpose.

I got into the car within ten minutes of getting your phone call. I got on to the motorway and got along pretty well at first, but the traffic was getting heavy as I got near Birmingham. Then I got a news flash on the radio that made me realise I'd got to change my route. I got on to a Services Area that had got an AA Office, where they advised me to get off the motorway at the next junction, because the traffic was getting worse the further south you got.

H

22 hardly

You must not add a negative (not, no, etc.) to *hardly*. It acts as a negative itself. (*Scarcely* acts in the same way.) So, you must not write (or say): "didn't hardly", "cannot scarcely", etc.

wrong

1 We *haven't hardly* enough petrol to get us home.
2 The committee *cannot scarcely* launch another appeal for funds so soon.
3 Her formal apology *didn't hardly* ring true, but it was accepted.

right

1 We've hardly enough petrol to get us home.
2 The committee can scarcely launch another appeal for funds so soon.
3 Her formal apology hardly rang true, but it was accepted.

23 he or him?

See also *I or me?/she or her?/they or them?/we or us?*

wrong

1 Fred knew that invitations were being sent to Bill, Eric and *he*, but he did not know whether they had yet been posted.
2 Pulchester's striker told our sports editor that three of his team mates and *him* are expecting to

be on the transfer list.

3 The chairperson is angry because the critics insist on blaming the team manager and *she* for the recent defeats.

4 That morning, to John's surprise, there were letters for Harry, Frank — a registered one — and *he*.

5 Richard was beaten in the final because Tom had trained harder than *him*.

6 Richard was beaten in the final because the crowd cheered Tom more than *he*.

right

1 Fred knew that invitations were being sent to Bill, Eric and him, but he did not know whether they had yet been posted.

2 Pulchester's striker told our sports editor that three of his team mates and he are expecting to be on the transfer list.

3 The chairperson is angry because the critics insist on blaming the team manager and her for the recent defeats.

4 That morning, to John's surprise, there were letters for Harry, Frank — a registered one — and him.

5 Richard was beaten in the final because Tom had trained harder than he.

6 Richard was beaten in the final because the crowd cheered Tom more than him.

Explanation

You make mistakes with *he* or *him* (*I* or *me/she* or *her/they* or *them/we* or *us*) when you let the words in between get in the way. If you strip the sentence down, you can see the sense of what you are writing.

1 You wouldn't write (or say) "— invitations were being sent to *he*", would you?
2 You wouldn't write (or say) "— *him* is expecting to be on the transfer list", would you?
3 You wouldn't write (or say) "— insist on blaming *she*", would you?
4 You wouldn't write (or say) "— there were letters for *he*", would you?

Sentences 5 and 6 show what happens when you forget what your sentences really mean. Here they are, with their meanings made plain:

5 Richard was beaten in the final because Tom had trained harder than he (had trained).
6 Richard was beaten in the final because the crowd cheered Tom more than (it cheered) him.

Practice

Fill each gap in the following sentences with either *he* or *him* according to the sense required.

1 James Brown wants to know whether there will be room for his two brothers and — to go with us in the car.
2 We can't possibly take the two of them, their luggage and — at the same time.
3 The young violinist was convinced that the judges were more impressed by his rival than — but his fears were not justified.

24 here is/here are: there is/there are

wrong

1 "Here *is* bargains at knockdown prices," as the stallholder said when he backed his lorry into his stall.
2 There *was*, the report said, clear signs throughout the country that the government was losing popularity.
3 There *are*, according to the forecasts, the prospect of settled weather for the harvest.

right

1 "Here are bargains — "
2 There were — clear signs —
3 There is — the prospect —

Practice

Fill each gap in the following sentences with *is* or *are* (or *was* or *were*) according to the sense required.

1 We got in too late to cook a proper meal, but there — milk and eggs in the fridge, so we didn't go hungry.
2 The doctor informed him that there — still some grounds for anxiety.
3 Here, if my calculations are right, — the obvious hiding place for coins.

I

25 *I* or *me*?

See also *he or him? she or her? they or them? we or us?*

There's nothing wrong with *me* — if *I'm* in the right place! People seem to think that *I* is somehow "better" than *me*; but *me* is often correct.

wrong

1 How nice! The Robinsons have invited Jenny and you and *I* to their Christmas party.
2 I must say, the annual choir outing was a great treat for my brothers and *I*.
3 This information has been given only to Johnson, Brown and *I*, so far.

right

1 How nice! The Robinsons have invited Jenny and you and me to their Christmas party.
2 I must say, the annual choir outing was a great treat for my brothers and me.
3 This information has been given only to Johnson, Brown and me, so far.

Explanation

It's the words "in between" that cause the mistake. If you remove them, you will know at once whether to write *I* or *me*.

1 You wouldn't write (or say) "The Robinsons have invited I to their Christmas party", would you?

2 You wouldn't write (or say) "— a great treat for I", would you?
3 You wouldn't write (or say) "— given to I", would you?

Practice

Fill each gap in the following sentences with *I* or *me* according to the sense required.

1 Most of the washing up had been done by us two boys, John and —, by the time John's parents returned.
2 We all went on holiday together last year, Peter, Mary and — .
3 There must be team changes before the next match, and I think the selectors will choose from Jane, if she's fit, Chris and — .

26 — it —

It (like *this* and *that* and *these* and *those* and *which*) must always be made to refer to something clear and definite that has gone before in the sentence.
If you forget that warning, you will write silly sentences, like this:

If your dog won't eat raw meat, cook it.

wrong
1 The failure of the maize crop was a disaster, for *it* kept the poor people alive.
2 Kathy's easy win in the competition surprised her teacher because *it* wasn't easy.

28

right

1 The maize crop kept the poor people alive, so its failure was a disaster.
2 Kathy's easy win in the difficult competition surprised her teacher.

Practice

Improve these sentences. Alter the wording of each sentence so that it makes clear sense. [Don't change the meaning.]

1 When your head is aching, a Magipill will put an end to it.
2 If your car has a puncture, blow it up.
3 He gave his last biscuit to the monkey because it was wet.
4 The council is reconsidering its decision to ban football on the estate because it is unpopular.

27 *its*

its is the possessive form of *it*

REMEMBER this sentence:
The cat is licking its paws.

28 *it's me*

it's means it is

See also *I or me*
In answer to the question, "Who's that?" the common form "It's me" (or just "Me") is all right *in speech*.

In writing, it is better to use the strictly accurate, "It is I".
And in sentences like these, always use *I* (or *he* or *she* or *we* or *they*) as the sense requires.

wrong

1 In the end, it was *me* who solved the problem.
2 To our surprise, it was *her* who was in possession of the missing papers.
3 Politicians forget that it is *us* voters who have to pay.

right

1 In the end, it was I who solved the problem.
2 To our surprise, it was she who was in possession of the missing papers.
3 Politicians forget that it is we voters who have to pay.

Practice

Select from the brackets the correct word to fill each gap in these sentences.

1 Extra points were awarded to six of — (us/we) junior entrants.
2 They were jeered at for being fussy about their lifejackets, but when the ship sank, it was — (them/they) who survived.
3 The officer would not permit my solicitor and — (I/me) to talk without a witness.

L

29 latter

The word must be used only to refer to one of *two* persons or things.
See also **former.**

wrong

1 Given a choice of beef, lamb or pork, she chose a joint of the *latter*.
2 Jane, Kay and Gwendolen were all in the running for promotion, but it was the *latter* who got the job in the end.

right

1 — a choice of lamb or pork, she ...
2 Kay and Gwendolen were in the running ...

30 *(to) lay or (to) lie?*

REMEMBER these sentences:

- You *lay* a table, but you *lie* on a bed.
- You *lay* a carpet, but it *lies* on the floor.
- You *lay* a trap, but it *lies* in its victim's path.

wrong

1 "*Lie* your guns down and *lay* on the floor," ordered the bandit.
2 I finished the washing early and had a *lay* down before tea.
3 She was *laying* there, half asleep, when the telephone rang.

4 We have *lain* a waterproof base to stop the damp coming through.

5 I have sometimes *laid* on the bed in the back room to get away from the noise from the street.

right

1 "Lay your guns down and lie on the floor," ordered the bandit.

2 I finished the washing early and had a lie down before tea.

3 She was lying there, half asleep, when the telephone rang.

4 We have laid a waterproof base to stop the damp coming through.

5 I have sometimes lain on the bed in the back room to get away from the noise from the street.

Explanation

● If you ask the question "What?" after the verb *to lay* you will find the answer in the sentence. For example:

Sentence You lay the table.
Question lay *what*?
Answer the table

If you ask the question "What?" after the verb *to lie* you will *not* find the answer in the sentence. For example:

Sentence You lie on the bed.
Question lie *what*?
Answer There is no answer: "on the bed" does not answer the question "lie *what*?" In fact, "lie *what*?" isn't a proper question. It doesn't make sense.

REMEMBER

If you are in doubt whether to write *lay* or *lie* ask the question *What?* after the verb. If there is an answer in the sentence, write *lay*. If there is not an answer in the sentence, write *lie*.

If you ask the question *Where?* after the verb *to lie* there may be an answer in the sentence. For example:

Sentence The books were lying on the floor.
Question were lying *where*?
Answer on the floor

If you ask the question *How?* after the verb *to lie* there may be an answer in the sentence. For example:

Sentence After roughing it in camp, it was a treat to be lying comfortably.
Question to be lying *how*?
Answer comfortably

REMEMBER these two sentences:
1. I *lay* the breakfast table each night before I go to bed.
2. I *lay* down and was soon asleep.

- Writers muddle *to lay* and *to lie* because those two words *look* the same, but are NOT the same.
  In 1 *lay* is the present tense of the verb *to lay*. (lay *what*? — the breakfast table)
  In 2 *lay* is a past tense of the verb *to lie*. (lay *what*? — no answer in the sentence: lay *how*? — down)

REMEMBER these two sentences:
1. They have laid the foundations of their new house.
2. They have lain in prison for six months.

In 1 *have laid* is a past tense of the verb *to lay*. (have laid *what*? — the foundations of their new house)
In 2 *have lain* is a past tense of the verb *to lie*. (have lain *what*? — no answer in the sentence: have lain *where*? — in prison)

Practice

Choose the correct word from the brackets to fill each gap in the following sentences:

1 That holiday, they spent their afternoons just — (laying/lying) in the sun.
2 When you — (lie/lay) the table in the corner, make sure that an extra place is — (lain/laid) for dinner tonight.
3 She isn't very well, but it's nothing that a cup of tea and a short — (lie/lay) down won't put right.
4 His cap was — (laying/lying) on the hall table, so we knew he was back, for he always — (lies/lays) it there when he comes in.

31 *less* or *few*?

Don't use *less* when you mean *few*.
Use *less* when you are referring to amount or bulk.
Use *few* when you are referring to numbers.

REMEMBER this sentence:
Because I was on a diet, I had to drink fewer cups of tea with less sugar in each.

wrong

1 The government won, but it had *less* votes than last time.
2 Our fuel stocks have been run down this winter, and we have in reserve *fewer* of either coal or wood than is safe.

right

1 — fewer votes —
2 — less of either coal or wood —

M

32 majority

Must be used *only* of numbers. It means "the greater number".

wrong

1 There were a few interesting pages, but the *majority* of the book was boring.
2 Mice got into the store and ate the *majority* of the grain.
3 Her bullying habits grew and cost her the *majority* of her support.

right

1 — most of the book —
2 — most of the grain —
3 — most of her support.

- Correct use of *majority*:

1 He had a majority of 1000 at the last election.
2 The majority of the pupils obey the rules.
3 Can we count on a majority in the committee?

33 *must of* misused for **must have**

The mistake is caused by the pronunciation of "must've", as in:

"I must've left my purse on the counter of that shop."

REMEMBER that "must've" means *must have* NOT *must of.*

The same mistake is made when people write *might of* and *could of.*

REMEMBER that "might've" means *might have* and "could've" means *could have.*

wrong

    1 We must *of* been mistaken.
    2 You might *of* taken more trouble.
    3 I could *of* caught an earlier train.

right

    1 We must have been mistaken.
    2 You might have taken more trouble.
    3 I could have caught an earlier train.

34 *myself* — *and all the other* "selves"

Don't write (or say) *myself* when you simply mean *I* or *me.* People who are not sure whether *I* or *me* is correct often try to dodge the problem by using *myself* instead.

wrong

    1 Peter's uncle asked Peter and *myself* to help him at the fete.
    2 The mechanic and *myself* patched up the engine at the roadside.
    3 The judges' decision surprised Kate and *myself,* but we had to accept it.

right

    1 Peter's uncle asked Peter and me to help him at the fete.
    2 The mechanic and I patched up the engine at the roadside.
    3 The judges' decision surprised Kate and me, but we had to accept it.

Explanation

You wouldn't write (or say):

1 Peter's uncle asked myself to help him.
2 Myself patched up the engine.
3 The judges' decision surprised myself.

Sometimes people write (or say) *myself* instead of *I* or *me* because they think it is somehow more "important" or more "dignified". It isn't! It's pompous when it's misused like that.

wrong

1 *Myself*, and the thousands who think like *myself*, will not rest until this injustice has been removed.
2 The committee insisted that *myself* — as captain of the first team — should make a speech at the dinner.

right

1 I, and the thousands who think like me, will not rest until this injustice has been removed.
2 The committee insisted that I — as captain of the first team — should make a speech at the dinner.

Here is the full list of the "self" words:
myself; yourself; himself; herself; itself; ourselves; yourselves; themselves.

Use them to show that the person or thing to which they refer is the same as a person or thing already named in the sentence. Like this:

right

1 The dog shook *itself* on the river bank.
2 Mrs Brown dressed *herself* quickly and hurried out of the house to catch her bus.
3 In the end, we decided to paint the house *ourselves*.

M

37

The "self" words are also used to emphasise a *contrast*. Like this:

1 My friends thought that my plan would not work, but I was confident myself.
2 His parents died young, but he lived to a ripe old age himself.
3 Everybody, except the travellers themselves, argued in favour of the new timetables.

N

35 neither

See also *either.*

Use *neither* only when you are referring to one of *two* persons or things. For three or more, use *none* or *not one*.

wrong

1 I went to the meeting with Sandy and Jane, but *neither* of us was impressed.
2 We interviewed five candidates — some very good — but *neither* was exactly right for the job, so we are re-advertising.

right

1 — but none of us was impressed.
2 — but not one was exactly right —

REMEMBER that *neither* and *neither of* must be followed by a singular verb. Like this:

I have asked both boys, but neither *is* willing to volunteer.
We stopped two passers-by, but neither *was* able to show us the way.

neither — nor

See *either — or* for the rules about the correct placing of these words in a sentence.

Is the verb after *neither — nor* singular or plural? You have to decide on the correct answer to that question each time you use *neither — nor*. Like this:

wrong

1 Neither Jane nor her father *have* blue eyes.
2 Neither our cousins nor their parents *answers* letters.
3 Neither their American friend nor the Browns *wants* to join in the picnic.
4 Neither the umpires nor the groundsman *think* that the ground is fit for play.
5 Neither they nor I *were* ready to agree.
6 Neither my friends nor I *are* in favour of the council's plan.

right

1 Neither Jane nor her father has blue eyes.
2 Neither our cousins nor their parents answer letters.
3 Neither their American friend nor the Browns want to join in the picnic.
4 Neither the umpires nor the groundsman thinks the ground is fit for play.
5 Neither they nor I was ready to agree.
6 Neither my friends nor I am in favour of the council's plan.

REMEMBER that the same rules apply to *either — or*.

Practice

Choose from the brackets the correct form of the verb to fill each gap in the following sentences.

1. It must be either my aunt or friends of hers who — (has/have) left that parcel in the porch.
2. While the old man was alive, neither his sons nor his wife — (were/was) allowed any say in running the business.
3. The weather has been so bad that neither the builders nor I — (are/am) confident that the roof will be on before winter.

36 nobody/no one

See also **anybody, any one,** etc.
Nobody and *no one* refer to *one* person (singular). All the words in the sentence that refer to *nobody* and *no one* must also be singular.

REMEMBER these sentences. They show the correct way of using *nobody* and *no one*.

1. Nobody can be a successful actress who *does* not do *her* best to help *her* colleagues in any company that *she* joins.
2. No one *is* wise to sign a legal document without first reading carefully all the clauses.

37 none

None may refer to *one* person or thing or to *more than one* person or thing, according to the sense of your sentence.

right

1. The tanker was full of oil when it ran aground, but none (no oil) *was* discharged.
2. The apples were stored so carefully that none (no apples) *were* rotten.

38 (a) number of

Usually (and sensibly) this expression is treated as being plural, nowadays.

right

1 A large number of these pupils *are* taking part in the cross-country race.
2 I planted a number of bulbs in that pot in the autumn and *they* bloomed at Christmas.

O

39 one — one

Don't switch from *one* to *you* or *he* or *they*, etc. If you start with *one*, stick to it until the sentence ends.

wrong

1 One should always carry a map and a compass when *you* are walking on the moorland.
2 In the beginners' class one was taught the correct way of looking after *their* equipment.

right

1 One should always carry a map and a compass when one is walking on the moorland.
2 In the beginners' class one was taught the correct way of looking after one's equipment.

REMEMBER that *one* is often an awkward expression. It is often better to avoid its use. The two sentences just used as examples would be better English if they were re-worded like this:

1 Walkers on the moorland should always carry a map and a compass.
or You should always carry a map and a compass when you are walking on the moorland.
2 In the beginners' class we were taught the correct way of looking after our equipment.

40 only

Be sure to put it in its right place in the sentence.

wrong

1 Ticket-holders can *only* get seats for this concert.
2 They said they would *only* repair the car if we paid a deposit before they started.
3 I *only* accepted her cheque because I trusted her.

right

1 Only ticket-holders can get seats for this concert.
2 They said they would repair the car only if we paid a deposit before they started.
3 I accepted her cheque only because I trusted her.

Explanation

Always ask yourself which word (or group of words) in the sentence *only* applies to. Then, when you have thought that out, place *only* as near to that word or group of words as possible.

Badly is another word that you have to think about. Like *only*, it has to go in to the right place, or you write nonsense.

wrong

1 He needs his hair cutting badly.
2 This house needs painting badly.
3 Your fans want you to sing another song badly.

right

1 He badly needs his hair cutting.
2 This house badly needs painting.
3 Your fans badly want you to sing another song.

P

41 paragraphs

A paragraph is a group of sentences that go together because each sentence in the group is about the same subject. Most pieces of writing – a letter or a composition, for example – are bound to contain several different subjects. They must, therefore, consist of several different paragraphs: one paragraph for each subject. *Unless a piece of writing is clearly divided into paragraphs it is very difficult for the reader to follow its meaning.* Starting a new paragraph is the writer's way of signalling to the reader that he is changing the subject.

- To show where a new paragraph begins, the first line starts about one inch (2 cm) in from the margin. This "indentation", as it is called, prepares the reader for the change of subject.

42 past/present/future – confused tenses

A sentence does not make sense when the tenses of the verbs jump about from present to past and past to future, etc. Confused tenses are often found in "may" and "might" and "should" and "would" sentences.

wrong

1 I *should* be pleased if you will let me have your answer next week.
2 You *would* be surprised by her performance when the results arrive.
3 Mr Jones *might* pass the driving test if he can improve his reversing techniques.
4 I think we *may* have upset him when we mentioned his previous employer, for they didn't get on.
5 If we do call for them, they *would* be astonished.

right

1 I shall be pleased if you will let me have your answer next week.
2 You will be surprised by her performance when the results arrive.
3 Mr Jones may pass the driving test if he can improve his reversing techniques.
4 I think we might have upset him when we mentioned his previous employer, for they didn't get on.
5 If we do call for them, they will be astonished.

Explanation

The tenses of the verbs in each of those sentences must be put "in balance" to make sense.

1 Future "I *shall* be pleased" balances something that belongs to the future: "if you will let me have".
2 Future "You *will* be surprised" balances something that belongs to the future: "when the results arrive".
3 Future "Mr Jones *may* pass" balances something that belongs to the future: "if he can improve".
4 Past "might *have* upset him" balances something that belongs to the past: "when we mentioned".
5 Future "they *will* be astonished" balances something that belongs to the future: "If we do call".

Those are simple, commonsense examples of the way to manage "the sequence of tenses". It is with sentences of those everyday patterns, using "may", "might", "should" and "would", that most mistakes are made. Once you are aware of the problem, you soon develop a sense of "what sounds right".

- Sudden shifts of tense from past to present, or present to future, and back again, make the writer's meaning difficult to follow.

P

R

43 reason/cause/because

These words are often used in a muddled way.

wrong

1 The reason *why* I cycle to work is to save money.
2 We discovered that the cause of the breakdown was *due to* a bare wire in the circuit.
3 The customers claimed that the reason they had been overcharged was *because* the new assistant did not know the proper prices.

right

1 *Either* I cycle to work to save money.
   Or The reason I cycle to work is to save money.
2 *Either* We discovered that the cause of the breakdown was a bare wire in the circuit.
   Or We discovered that the breakdown was due to a bare wire in the circuit.
   Or We discovered that the breakdown was caused by a bare wire in the circuit.
3 *Either* The customers claimed that the reason they had been overcharged was that the new assistant did not know the proper prices.
   Or The customers claimed that they had been overcharged because the new assistant did not know the proper prices.

S

44 scarcely

See *hardly*

45 sentences — *six common faults*

1 Cut-off sentences — full stop too soon

REMEMBER Sentences must not stop until they have finished!

wrong
1 In reply to your letter. There are no vacancies in July.
2 It will be a poor apple crop. Chiefly because of the late frosts.
3 Things were bad, but the captain put on a cheerful face. To encourage his crew.

right
1 In reply to your letter, we have to inform you that there are no vacancies in July.
2 Chiefly because of the late frosts, it will be a poor apple crop.
3 Things were bad, but the captain put on a cheerful face to encourage his crew.

2 Run-on sentences — full stop too late

REMEMBER Sentences must not run on after they have finished!

R
S

wrong

1 June had a camera for Christmas at Easter she bought some filters.

2 I must garden this weekend after all the fine weather may not last.

3 The blizzard was unexpected in half an hour the main road was blocked by evening the power lines were down.

right

1 June had a camera for Christmas. At Easter she bought some filters.

2 I must garden this weekend. After all, the fine weather may not last.
   or
   I must garden this weekend, after all. The fine weather may not last.

3 The blizzard was unexpected. In half an hour the main road was blocked. By evening the power lines were down.

3 Split sentences — words wedged into the wrong places

REMEMBER Don't split the subject away from the verb by wedging other words in between them.

wrong

1 The blind man's dog, although you will find this hard to believe, knew exactly when to get his master off the bus.

2 Our schooldays, my sister and I were talking about them last night, were not at all unhappy, though they, whatever people are fond of saying, were not the happiest days of our lives.

3 The travellers owing to the noise from the airfield and their uncomfortable beds did not get a lot of sleep that night.

right

1 Although you will find this hard to believe, the blind man's dog knew exactly when to get his master off the bus.

2 Last night, my sister and I were talking about our schooldays, which were not at all unhappy, though they were not the happiest days of our lives, whatever people are fond of saying.

3 Owing to the noise from the airfield and their uncomfortable beds, the travellers did not get a lot of sleep that night.

Explanation

A good sentence says two things quickly and clearly:

- first, it tells the reader who or what its subject is;
- second, it tells the reader something about that subject – what it is doing, or what is happening to it. Anything that interrupts that flow of information weakens the sentence.
- Words pushed in between the subject and its verb clog up the meaning.

4 Mish-mash sentences — word groups jumbled up

REMEMBER The words that make sense *together* must be placed *close together* in the sentence.

wrong

1 Wanted immediately — three-bedroomed house by business woman within easy reach of the station.

2 My cousin fancied the coat in Blake's window made of Angora wool last week.

3 The guard commanded the prisoner to sit down in an angry voice.

4 He realised that his watch was slow with a shock and that he would be late for his appointment while he was cleaning his teeth.

S

5 Fluttering brightly in the sunshine, the visitors were delighted by the carnival decorations.

right

1 Wanted immediately by business woman – three-bedroomed house within easy reach of the station.
2 My cousin fancied the coat made of Angora wool that was in Blake's window last week.
3 In an angry voice, the guard commanded the prisoner to sit down.
4 While he was cleaning his teeth, he realised with a shock that his watch was slow and he would be late for his appointment.
5 The visitors were delighted by the carnival decorations fluttering brightly in the sunshine.

5 Squinting sentences — "pointing out" words that don't point out

REMEMBER When *it*, *that*, *this*, *these*, *those*, and *which* are used to point at (or refer to) another word or group of words, they must be used so that they point clearly and accurately to *one particular word* or *one particular group of words*. The reader must not be left wondering what it is that a "pointing out" word is pointing out!

wrong

1 The speaker reminded her audience that the company had enjoyed a successful year in spite of the managing director's absence through illness and said she knew how pleased they all were by that.
2 The jack plug must be connected to the co-axial lead from the output socket. This is not supplied with the kit, but may be obtained as an extra.
3 Taking care to disturb the roots as little as possible, the plants should be removed from the containers which must then be buried 18 inches deep.

right

1 Reminding her audience that the company had enjoyed a successful year in spite of the managing director's absence through illness, the speaker said she knew how pleased they all were by that success.

2 The jack plug, which is not supplied with the kit but may be obtained as an extra, must be connected to the co-axial lead from the output socket.

3 Having been removed from the containers with as little root disturbance as possible, the plants must then be buried 18 inches deep.

6 Dithering sentences — switching from one track to another

REMEMBER When a writer begins a sentence in one way and then switches to another way before it is finished, the sentence becomes confused – and so does the reader!

wrong

1 This is the station *from* which we set out *from* on that rotten journey.

2 When the manager gave him a revised bill, he saw that it contained the same item *to* which he had objected *to* in the first place.

3 You should have seen the state *in* which the previous occupants had left the caravan *in*.

right

1 *Either* "— from which we set out —" *or* "—which we set out from —".

2 *Either* "— to which he had objected —" *or* "— which he had objected to —".

3 *Either* "— in which the previous occupants had left the caravan —" *or* "— which the previous occupants had left the caravan in —".

S

REMEMBER A similar muddle often occurs when the words *height*, *rainfall* and *temperature* are used. Writers often forget which track they started out on and switch to another before the sentence ends.

wrong

1 The *height* of the chimney is 45 metres *high*.
2 The *rainfall* of the counties west of the Pennines is *wetter* than that of the counties to the east.
3 The *temperature* of the protective casing was becoming dangerously *hot*.

right

1 The chimney is 45 metres high. *or* The height of the chimney is 45 metres.
2 The rainfall of the counties west of the Pennines is greater than that of the counties to the east. *or* The counties to the west of the Pennines are wetter than those to the east.
3 The temperature of the protective casing was becoming dangerously high. *or* The protective casing was becoming dangerously hot.

46 *she or her?*

See also *he or him? I or me? they or them? we or us?*

wrong

1 Janet always believed that her brothers were treated more favourably than *her*.
2 The prize went to Jean, but Ann consoled herself with the thought that the audience applauded the winner less enthusiastically than *she*, the runner-up.

right

   2   — were treated more favourably than she (was treated).
   3   — the audience applauded the winner less enthusiastically than (it applauded) her, the runner-up.

47 subject/verb — singular *or* plural

wrong

   1 A list of books recently added to the library *have* been posted on the notice board.
   2 The aid of a dictionary, a grammar book and his parents *were* needed when Tom wrote his letter of application.
   3 A case of empty Coke bottles *were* put out after the party.

right

   1 A list of books — has been posted —
   2 The aid of a dictionary, a grammar book and his parents was needed —
   3 A case of empty Coke bottles was put out —

Explanation

The writer went wrong because he failed to recognise the subject.

   1 Subject: *list*. Verb: *has been posted*.
   2 Subject: *aid*. Verb: *was needed*.
   3 Subject: *case*. Verb: *was put out*.

S

T

48 tenses

See *past/present/future*.

49 — that —

See *— it —* and **sentences**.

50 their or there?

Use *their* to show possession.
Use *there* to show direction, position, place.

REMEMBER these sentences:
There was no way now in which they could escape *their* pursuers. So, *there* they were, overtaken by *their* fate, at last.

51 they or them?

See also **he or him? I or me? she or her? we or us?**

wrong
1 It looks as if it was *them* who broke into the warehouse.
2 It was not an easy choice to make between you, the bright but lazy applicants, on the one hand, and *they*, the hard-working but not very intelligent candidates, on the other.

right

    1 — it was *they* who broke into —
    2 — between you, the bright but lazy applic-
       ants — and (between) *them* —

Explanation

    1 You wouldn't write (or say) "Them broke into the
      warehouse", would you?
    2 You wouldn't write (or say) "between they",
      would you?

52 — this —

    See — *it* — and **sentences**.

W

53 we or us?

See also *he* or *him? I* or *me? she* or *her? they* or *them?*

wrong

1 I've seen the travelling arrangements, and you and *us* are starting at different times.
2 There will be a hot meal in camp for the early arrivals and a cold supper for *we* others who get in late.

right

1 — you and we are starting —
2 — for us others —

Explanation

1 You wouldn't write (or say) "us are starting", would you?
2 You wouldn't write (or say) "a cold supper for we", would you?

Practice

Choose from the brackets the correct word to fill each gap in the following sentences.

1 It's goodbye from my colleague, John Smith, and — (I/me) until next week.
2 You can't possibly get them, with all their baggage, and — (we/us) into one car.
3 They were kind enough to invite our grandparents and — (we/us) to pay them a visit next summer.

54 were or was?

Sometimes it is right to use *were* where *was* might be expected. This happens in "If" sentences.

wrong

1 If I *was* you I'd go by train.
2 She'd be just right for that part if only she *was* a few years younger.
3 If my surname *was* Stinks, I'd change it.

right

1 If I were you, I'd go by train.
2 She'd be just right for that part if only she were a few years younger.
3 If my surname were Stinks, I'd change it.

Explanation

When the "if words" introduce a purely imaginary condition – one extremely unlikely to be true – use *were*.

1 — but I'm *not* you, and I can't be – so, *were*
2 — but she *isn't* a few years younger, and she can't be – so, *were*
3 — but my surname isn't Stinks, and it can't be – so, *were*

REMEMBER Use *were* instead of *was* ONLY when the condition is so unlikely as to be practically impossible. When the condition is a likely one, use *was*.

right

1 If that was the paper boy at the door, ask him to wait.
2 I shall miss my bus if that was eight .o'clock striking.
3 If that was a mouse in the larder I shall buy a trap.
4 When I rang the bell they asked if I was calling for the jumble.

W

Practice

Fill each gap in the following sentences with either *was* or *were*.

1 She said she wouldn't marry him if he — a king.
2 The secretary of the club asked if I — a member.
3 If I — a saint he'd try my patience.

55 who *or* whom?

The rules are not kept as strictly as they used to be. Nowadays, most people say (and write), "Who did you see?" instead of the strictly accurate, "Whom did you see?" But there are still "rights" and "wrongs".

wrong

1 Thompson is the runner *whom* I think will win.
2 The new boss, *who* everyone detested, was moved on.
3 We must have seen the man *who* the policeman described.
4 Gloria was the star *who* the crowds flocked to see.
5 It was my first coach to *who* I owed my later success.

right

1 Thompson is the runner who I think will win.
2 The new boss, whom everyone detested, was moved on.
3 We must have seen the man whom the policeman described.
4 Gloria was the star whom the crowds flocked to see.
5 It was my first coach to whom I owed my later success.

Explanation

Use *who* when it is the subject of a verb. In all other cases, use *whom*.

W

Answers to Practice Exercises

4 1 already 2 all ready

6 1 altogether 2 all together

8 1 his – his 2 does – his – himself 3 is – himself – is

15 1 Wrong.Move *both*: '... expect both to ...' 2 Wrong.Move *either*: '... for either they ...'

21 for example: the last sentence – drove had leave getting went

23 1 him 2 him 3 him

24 1 were 2 were 3 is

25 1 me 2 I 3 me

26 1 ... to the pain. 2 ... blow the tyre up. 3 Because his last biscuit was wet, he gave it to the monkey. 4 ... its unpopular decision ...

28 1 us 2 they 3 me

30 1 lying 2 lay – laid 3 lie 4 lying – lays

35 1 have 2 was 3 am

53 1 me 2 us 3 us

54 1 were 2 was 3 were